persona non grata

by
Christopher
Michael

COVER PHOTO BY NICK RAD PHOTOGRAPHY
DESIGNED AND EDITED BY DANNY (DNY) STRACK
ADDITIONAL EDITS BYJESSICA VIDAL HARRIS, ANGIE SMITH
&VICTORIA MURRAY
INTERIOR ARTWORK BY MADISON THOMAS

EDITIO PRINCEPS

First Edition Printed May 2015
by Austin Slam Poetry Publishing

DEDICATIONE

This book is dedicated to those in the community who inspired the writing between these pages:

Doc, Scott Free, Angel, JVZ, Danez Smith, Cousin Sarah, Kylie, Zai, Babatunde, B-Young, Queen Pen, John Crow, B-Young, Marquise Mobley, Glori-B, Buddy Wakefield, B-Fran, Jesse Parent, Jamaal St. John, Good Ghost Bill, Mal, Chucky Black, Element 615, Phetote, Eugenia, April Freya, Tova, Shake, Chris Chrown & Brandon Michael

GRATIA

To Danny Strack for getting me off my butt and making this book happen.

To Mathew John Conley for inspiring me to write Haiku and Jacob Dodson for being the example to follow.

To my homes away from home: Under One Roof, Killeen Poetry Slam, Austin Poetry Slam, & Austin Neo Soul

Thank you Lord for this talent and I pray someone is touched by the words you bless me with.

CONTENTA

– PART 4 –
EMERITUS

– PART 5 –
CONSENSU

– PART 6 –
PERSONA NON GRATA

Et Al – "And others."

Et Cetera – "And the rest." And so on.

Ex Gratia – "From grace." Voluntarily performing an act purely out of kindness,

Ex Post Facto – "From a thing done afterward." A law with retroactive effect.

Fiat Lux – "Let there be light."

Fortes in Fide – "Strong in faith."

Gloria in Excelsis Deo – "Glory to God in the Highest."

Habeas Corpus – "You have the body."

In Absentia – "In the absence."

In Situ – "In the place." In the original place or approp

In Vitr

In Vivo

Ipso Fa

Magna

Magnu piece of an artist's career.

Malum in Se – "Bad in itself." A thing that is inherently wrong.

Malum Prohibitum – "Bad by prohibition." A thing that is only wrong because it is illegal.

Mater Dei – "Mother of God." Mary, who gave birth to Jesus.

Mea Culpa – "Through my fault."

Modus Operandi – "Method of operating."

Mutatis Mutandis – "After changing what needed to be changed."

Non Sequitur – "It does not follow." A thing that is absurd because it is out of context

Omnia Vincit Amor – "Love conquers all."

Opus Dei – "The Work of God."

Para Bellum – "Prepare for war."

– PART 1 –
FIAT LUX
"Let there be light."

HAI·KU
俳句

THERE ARE NO CHAIRS IN MY MIND.
I'M SCARED ALZHEIMER'S MIGHT TRY TO SIT
IN.

ADAM

From the moment light breathed life into this dirt I've been
trying to shake the dust off my heels.

It's hard to believe I walked with El Shaddai
and could not feel a sense of sufficient satisfaction.

Sometimes I wonder if maybe I'm plugged into the matrix,
still sleepin' and death is waking up with an appreciation for
Eden.

I begged for a pardon from the endless loneliness of tending
His garden. Saddened by my plight Jehovah-Jireh, felt it not
right that I be alone.

Eyes closed, laid rest,
Elohim digging in the deepness of my seams,
I slept so he could find the woman of my dreams.

> *It wasn't me there first.*
> *It's always been you and me.*
> *Even when we was just me.*

I guess you were hiding in the bones that guard my heart.
There's been moments when I'd rather just have the rib back
but either way I'm incomplete without you.

I remember the softness of your hands,
the sweetness of the sin you handed me
and the pungent aroma of the revelation of information that
flooded my faculties.
I'm not blaming you. But...

Devils don't have to dance in the dark when they can disguise
themselves as snakes and bitter friends.

Satan sings like a siren knowing his venomous sap-like song will seep into your soul so slow you won't see it coming.

Maybe you should spend less time listening to fallen angels bending your ear in angles that make it hard for you to hear me.

I LOVE YOU!

I stand in the gap between your wrong and Love's wrath cause I know that even a cursed earth would be easier to traverse if I had both my halves to navigate the narrow path.

Eden would be nothing,
without the other side of me,
thee, Eve.

This way Yahweh's gotta go through me to get to you.
So I sank my teeth into forbidden fruit on purpose,
protecting you is my new purpose,
baby, you are worth this.

I never told you this but Abba first offered me an angel.
Well, I don't date outside my race.
Not loving the dirt, is not loving myself.
Clay, soil or sand I don't really give a damn,
I don't want angels, I want you my Eve, my woman,
my fellow human, I love you and all your colors.

Let me tell you this:
*I don't wear clothes cause I'm ashamed of my
nakedness,
I'm trying to hide cause I realize that Lu was just
jealous of me and you. He is the father of lies
don't let that fool deceive you, OUR actions are
what he wants,
so we can fall too!*

9

I KNOW AN ANGEL

Sometimes Angels give up their wings to live among us.
Perhaps they envy life among us dirt preferring green
grass, over gold streets.

I know an Angel
and even with out her forfeited feathered phalanges
she floats into a room she's super...
Natural,
like the super soft naps on her crown
she's a queen.

Forsakes her wings but hides her halo in her smile.
Heaven hovers in her words.
She encourages me with just a hello.
Her hugs warm me from the inside out.

But
the problem with pure personalities preferring to be people
playing in the dirt is that the soil our souls sit in has been
corrupted,
subjected to frailties since the fall.

If we're not fighting our flesh
it's fighting us,
all out war!
The Geneva Convention should consider cancer a war crime,
a weapon of mass destruction.
The only counter attacks we have poisons the very ground
we're trying to take back.

Chemo causes the crowns of kings and queens to crack and
crumble.

Our earth has low self esteem, unable to accept better.

We have a tendency to reject the best.

Ask the Lamb and the Lion of Judah.

Maybe her body is rejecting her,

cause she
            is too good
                        for us...

GONE

She...is the daughter of the greatest mother ever.

Loving
Compassionate
And clever
Wise enough to be a magnificent mother
But young enough to be an even better...friend
Often mistaken for twins
Until...the forgetting begins

At first it was little things like
Location of car keys
And key ingredients to favorite recipes
Now all Mom sees
Strangers
In the faces she helped form

Blank stares
Empty glares reveal the reflection of the shadow of a vulture
Picking at her mom's memories
Her moments in life
Can't remember being a daughter
A mother
A wife
Her mother has forgotten more than most people ever knew
As the magical moments of lucidity become few
Praying for strength is all her little girl can do

One by one mom's memories fall away like the pedals of a
flower
Without the hope of new blossoms come spring
Her first kiss... gone
First love...   gone
Favorite movie...   gone

Some say stress caused her daughters headaches
Or was it the pain of a brain being swollen with the memories of
watching her mom's mind being stolen?

Forced to watch fate shake the etch-a-sketch of a mind
A cruel joke
Erasing her most precious times
Her daughter's first word...
Gone
Wedding day...   gone
Favorite prayer...   gone

And all you can offer this little girl
Are hollow words of hope
Like
Don't worry, it's gonna be OK
beause one day the great redeemer will bring her home
And renew her mind
She will once again remember those good times
But in the meantime
Her brain must be the valley
because death is casting a shadow
That won't let her see her own thoughts

Think about it.
It's metaphysically impossible for you to imagine what it's like
not to know what you're thinking about
because you have to be able to think to imagine

So just imagine dying from the inside out
Your hands won't put the food in your mouth
because your brain doesn't have enough clout
Stuck in a dream and you don't even know how to shout

A brilliant star...collapsing under the weight of her own gravity
Pulling everything in
So no thought can escape the eternal darkness

13

It would be opposite of Multiple Sclerosis or Parkinson's
I wonder which is worse
Being locked in a body with limbs still trying
Or trapped by life
While family watches your brain...dying

How to drive...   gone
How to read...   gone
How to cook...   gone

The scene has become routine
Daughter finds mom in the hall surrounded by family photos
The details of freshly water colored faces
are running off the canvas of her memory like wet paint
Frantic and panicked
Confused and dazed can't remember where she is most days
Shortly after sunset... you can look in mom's eyes and see the
holes in her mind
As all her bad and good times slowly swiss cheeses and rewinds
Her lifetime is reduced to a reel-to reel movie on a projector
stuck in one spot too long
As frame after frame warps, bubbles, and melts away
under the intense light
of old timer's...

Alzheimer's disease

How to laugh.
                    Gone
How to love.
                              Gone
Her daughter's name......

14

#BRINGBACKOURPENS

In 2014 over 200 schoolgirls in Nigeria were kidnapped
sparking a viral outrage of tweets and reposts.

#bringbackourgirls

When was the last time you lost your cell phone?
Have you ever misplaced your keys?
When you do, you scour your house.
You excavate the junk in your car, you up end your purse,
and pat your pockets.

When your keys are missing you don't run to your neighbor's
house to help them find theirs.

When you think your phone has slipped between the caverns of
your car seats you don't check for a stranger's missing phone, in
a random car, in some other parking lot.

When you suspect your ID card, your $20 bill, your favorite
medium ball point black ink pen, has been kidnapped,
you don't walk out your own door, cross the border,
ocean your way to another continent and focus on the missing
black ink in another's purse or pocket,
pretending you never lost your own black ink.

Is it American amnesia that silences your own loss?
Is it ignorance or fear
that forces glaucoma to form over your own vision?

Is that why you can't see the missing black ink
writing on your own wall?

Or is it that amber alerts can only reflect
against the backdrop of a white page?

Is it 'cause white paper missing from America's notebook is powerfully more noticeable than a handful of black ink pens? White page, only 2/5ths as good, without black pens.

Someone is always walking off with our black pens.
Call it vanishing ink.
Just another black Bic!

In 2013, 170,000 black children went missing in America.
Sparking... Nothing.
#blackandmissingfoundation

When was the last time you lost your cell phone?
Have you ever misplaced your keys?
When you do you scour your house.
You excavate the junk in your car, you up end your purse, and pat your pockets.

You don't tweet about it,
you be about it.

You look everywhere for them,
and you don't stop till you find them.

You phone a friend,
you assign blame,
you stop,
you refocus,
you beg God to show you that missing thing,
but you never stop looking,
and you don't concentrate on your neighbor's problems
until you fix your own.

#bringbackourpens

FOR SARAH

She came to me with eyes like glasses of milk with her own little
Earth floating in them.

The coldness of her situation must be causing condensation
around them, 'cause she was leaking her pain all over me.

When one of her tears rolled onto my heart
the only thing I knew to do was hug her.
Squeeze her as if I had the strength to force out every drop of
her salty circumstances from the corners of those big blue
planets that pass for eyes.

Girl was getting railroaded.

She honored me by trusting me,
believing I had the ability to navigate her down the tracks
of her pain, like I was some sort of Harriet Tubman that could
cast a light on unfamiliar ground
and help her to emotional freedom.

Baby daddy is feeling the spirit of giving
so he wants her to involuntarily donate time with her seed
so his girlfriend's momma can play granny.

Against the ropes,
she, Muhammad Ali,
he, Joe Frasier,
pounding away at her
with his son wrapped around his fist
like a twisted boxing glove
illegally weighted with the threat of litigation
and the fear of losing one more minute
with the one man she swears she'll make better than his daddy.

It's no wonder her moat is filled with crocodiles
and her castle doors kept closed.
'Cause he's trying to steal the one treasure she has left from
their relationship
using her son as a battering ram.
She's not trying to protect herself,
she has the walls raised to keep from hurting those left in her
life she can still bear to love.

What I wanted to tell her was I'm sorry cousin,
I have no experience in your situation
'cause there was never a temptation to hurt her with them.

Why harm the woman who helps me mould my boys to men,
one made of us
and the other only one step away from being her own child.
The demise of our marriage saw the rise of a better relationship.

By the time the papers were filed we were best friends.
No need for our children to suffer because our romance came
to an end.

We might have bruises on our hearts
but they sure as hell didn't come from using our children as
lawn darts.

We are gardeners entrusted with seeds that need the
nourishment and support provided by mom and dad.

That's what I wanted to say.
After all it's the truth.

Instead I'll say this.
No man can manufacture enough manure
to extinguish your flame...

Cousin you are a star!

A self-sustained nuclear reaction.

You give life and light the way,
you give seeds something to look up to and reach for.
Your touch makes flowers blossom and reveal their beauty.

You are mom!

So smile, 'cause without you,
that moon of a man would have no glow
and sooner or later your son will see on his own,
his father is just a lifeless rock floating in the darkness.

She wiped the condensation from her face
as the star in her smile warmed the room.

There's nothing he can do to take your seed away.

Then I hugged her.
                Told her,

        let's forget tomorrow
                            and enjoy the day.

WORKING TITLE FOR MOM POEM

This poem is dedicated to my mother, and is titled:

"Mom"
or
"Mother"
or
"thank you for being my mother"
or
"thank you for being my father"
or
"thank you for not trying to be my friend"
or
"thank you for making me think we were rich and never
letting me see the financial struggle on your face"
(you hid it well but I know better now)
or
"look what my mother made!"
or
"the woman that painted my picture but trusted me to color
it in"
or
"I'd like to believe I was worth your struggle"
or
"thank you for still being there for me"
or
"thank you for still being here for me"
or
"I love you Mom!"

OPEN LETTER #1 – LOVE LETTER TO SOL

I count my days with your departure and
arrival.

You are the sun that opens the flowers, warms
the day, lights the way and makes the moon
worth looking at.

Orbiting your love I am the Earth,
an abused celestial entity with too many holes
in my ozone… the rays of your affection are
sometimes more than I can handle.

Your gravity pulls me in spinning around you
but I can't move any closer than I am of fear I
will be overwhelmed consumed and vaporized by
the one thing you give me that matters most,
that thing that keeps me alive. I can't give in
and commit,
I don't want these ice caps to melt and I can't
let you go either. How will my flowers grow?

Conflicted,
confused,
convinced and unsure,
in love,
in fear,
I'm sorry if I seem so bipolar.

But you keep me spinning on my axis.
Even though I've been over run and over
populated by those selfishly stripping me of
all I have to give 'cause they thought it was
an inexhaustible resource.

The high pressure and low pressure systems of
my head and heart clash trying to purge me of
the monsters that have mangled my surface,
striving to shake them off with record level
magnitudes but they don't get it.

I dread the rare moments when the lifeless
remnants of my past eclipse the warm light of
your love thankful it doesn't last long.

You always manage to chase the clouds away and
brighten my horizons.

I hope you remember no matter how distant,
you've got to believe there's life out here.

One day you'll get tired.
Whatever universal magic fuels the rays of life
that caresses me every day will burn out.
You'll shrink away,
then supernova
and when you do...
take what's left of me with you.

23

that continues until everyone is sick of it.

Ad Perpetuam Memoriam – "To the perpetual memory"

Alias – "At another time, otherwise." An assumed identity.

Alibi – "Elsewhere." To be somewhere else during a crime.

Alma Mater – "Nourishing mother." Your school.

Alte

Bell

Bon

Can

Car

Chr

– PART 2 –
AD NAUSEAM
"To the point of disgust."

Cogito Ergo Sum – "I think therefore I am."

Consensu – "With consent."

Corpus Christi – "Body of Christ."

Cum Laude – "With praise."

Cura Personalis – "Care for the whole person."

Curriculum Vitae – "Course of life." Overview of a life and deeds.

De Facto – "By Deed."

Deus Ex Machina – "God from the machine."

Dramatis Personæ – "The parts of the play." Characters in a drama.

E Pluribus Unum – "Out of many, one."

Editio Princeps – "First edition." The first printed edition of a work.

Emeritus – "Veteran." The position held at the point of retirement, as an honor.

Ergo – "Therefore."

Et Al – "And others."

Et Cetera – "And the rest." And so on.

Ex Gratia – "From grace." Voluntarily performing an act purely out of kindness,

HAI·KU
俳句

TO THOSE WHITE FOLKS WHO SAY
"I'M COLOR BLIND"
DOES THAT MEAN YOU CAN'T SEE ME?

THEY, RIOT OVER CHAMPIONSHIPS
WE, RIOT OVER INJUSTICE

TRUTH IS A PIECE OF CLAY
TO BE MOLDED BY THE WINNER
HISTORY

SEEDS

It's brilliant!

How nature moves through the breeze,
seductively stroking trees,
forth, back
and forth again,
until gravity and the wind forces the mighty behemoth to
release its seed.
Mother Earth opens to receive,
soil embraces seed and life proceeds quietly in her womb.

A slow and arguably sexy process so we can have memories of
he likes she embossed with heart etched in bark.

See the leaves basking solar rays in summer days.
Fathom...
how they photosynthesize to preserve their lives.
They breathe,
breaking bonds of carbon dioxide allowing us to oxygenize.

So we can behold the autumned beautiful browns,
summered gorgeous greens
and the rainbow of crayoned leaves in between.
So we can feed, breath, read.

Home of the sparrow you keep your eye on and the morning
bird that trumpets the arrival of our closest star.

Oak and maple
make marvelous puppet masters
for deep dark chocolate mocha marionettes.

Let us never forget.

Strong Geppetto arms pulling the strings of Pinocchio picnicked
Negros air dancing for faces uncolored by Crayola,
deprived of the joy of coloring outside their lines.
Entertained by flailing fruit,
I never understood...
how a sight so common could have ever been considered
strange.

I guess they were in good company 'cause the renamed savior I
serve was sacrificed across an altar of wood...

Trees.

Their life gives life,
protection from the elements,
skin and bones for our homes.
The mighty mast for sails and bows on boats
ever buoyant keeping afloat,
safely transporting deeply pigmented savages through the
middle passages.

From cargo aboard ships stacked with no room,
to head honchos running board rooms.
We have come a long way...
but we have not arrived.

Having a black president has not stopped the cops from taking
our lives.

Too bad bullets aren't made of seeds,
so every time a black man wrongfully catches one
he could be the foundation from which it springs
instead of air dancing beneath its leaves
                                    gasping for breath
                    wishing he had been born with wings.

        Our holocaust us generations!

But I refuse...
to allow the burden of "mystory" to weigh me down,
or stand on it...
like a pitiful excuse to barely rise above mediocrity.
But I'll be damned if I'll allow you...
to tell me...
to get over it.

Nor will I allow the world to forget,
        our holocaust us generations.

It's beautiful,
How nature quietly moves in the breeze,
seductively stroking trees,
forth, back
and forth again,
until gravity and the wind...
                    I wonder

        If trees were aware that they were tools of terror,
would they still release their seed?

FIRE HOSE

The steady drip of water can wear down a rock
or reshape a mountain.

A fire hose can create a directed blast of water
that measures upwards of 400 pounds per square inch.
That's equivalent to the full concentrated weight of a male
gorilla standing in a space too small for even a pawn on a
chessboard.

The fire hose
is used to extinguish a flame before its heat can be felt.
Before the flame leaves its telltale **black** scorch marks.

A pressure washer
is used to clean the **black** and grime off walls.
It's used on sidewalks to wash away dead leaves, animal feces or
the **black**ened stains left by our machines.

Fire hoses have also been used to extinguish the flame of a
people whose fire was ignited by a desire to be equal,
they dared to march in streets until their heat could be felt.

Pressure washers or "water cannons" are used to wash away the
black and drown out the voice.
It can flick a man off his feet like
                            check
                                    mate,
they killed our King.

You can see video of such cannons hurling droplets with the
weight of 400-pound gorillas,
cleaning sidewalks and city streets of people
like the **black** of them is a stain to be removed
with all the reverence afforded to dead leaves and animal shit.

NEVER FORGET!!

Life is a curious thing.

Animal feces are essential in the spreading and germination of some seeds.

The decay of dead things feeds the tallest trees and the deepest grass roots.

Water hoses can also bring the fluid of life to the most barren of places.

Did you know,
that the stench of feces and decaying things is flammable?

Keep killing us.
Keep shitting on us.
You are only making us stronger,
and eventually there will not be enough material to create the hoses to contain the water needed to put out our flame.

DON'T

By the grace of God I've never had to live life in a closet.
Instead, I am the closet turned inside out,
wearing the shadow of closed closets weaved in my skin,
every day. A clear reflection of lights out,
the darkness that is now quietly feared, secretly hated,
cause public ridicule of Negros is now taboo.
Progress!

The world is changing but just in case it isn't fast enough
here's some advice.

You gotta Cotton Club,
shuck and jive.

Even when reminding one how difficult it is to be black,
how deadly it is to be black,
how privileged one is not to be...
Your expertly trained feet can distract by dancing a jig.
Watch me Mary Poppins you with a spoon full of sugar.

White face at work,
                smile,
                     show your teeth,
        your teeth are white they can identify with that.

Make them laugh you cannot hate and laugh simultaneously.

                              Don't take too much credit.
            Don't be on time.
Be early.
        Don't be seen,
                be heard,
                        they love our music...
but won't pay to see us in the theater.

When they do you wrong...
and you will be done wrong (it is the nature of mankind)
you can't get as angry as they would.
Our angry is amplified
by the commercialized crumbs of our culture.

We **don't** have lobbyists paying politicians and producers
to protect
our persona
is poisoned
by popular cable news entertainment of us
committing all the crimes.

Their vision of us is tainted by the jungles of Africa
they think they see on TV.

*Flared nostrils on an already broad nose looks like the beast
before it strikes.*

Righteously enraged and reddened eyes against your brown
brick skin looks like a house ablaze and you know folks love a
good burning.

Hence it's safer to yell fire than to yell rape.

Calm down
Don't be the beast they've been warned about.
Your justified outrage over wrongdoing will look like you're
climbing Empire State Buildings, swatting planes with one hand
while clutching a white woman in the other.
AAAAaaaarrrgh!!

SON don't let them King Kong you!

Don't let your hair do anything they can't appropriate.

Don't do the latest cultural hand-to-hand greeting in public
unless they've allowed it passage on the mainstream.

Don't think your acceptance on the court
will get us equality in the courts.

    Don't confuse success on the football field and honor on the
                              battlefield with freedom from the cotton field.

Even, if you're the duly elected, electoral college selected,
president of the greatest, the freest country in the world,
you must maintain your composure.

So when the gentlemen of the senate break protocol and
centuries of tradition to yell obscenities at you during a speech,
you must shackle your desire to retort.

Noose your need to go Chicago half nigga upside his head.

Whip your face into shape, oversee your reactions, be the massa
of your emotions.

                                         Don't sweat.
                                  Don't flinch;
    keep your eyes on the TelePrompTer BOY!

Most of all,
you must allow them privilege of not realize they are staring
inside the closet.

                        The closet their grandparents
               have hidden their family skeletons in.

    Those memories will make them hate you more.

Remember,
memory loss is the only reparations they will ever offer you.

OPEN LETTER #2 – AFRO-LIFE

Brothers & Sisters:

Do you believe in the Afro-life? Has your soul been picked? Are you frustrated with the permanence of your temporary situation? Can't pay your bills because your ends are split?
Unhappy with the highlights of your life?

Well, dread-knot my friend!
When things get grey you don't have to get twisted.

Here at the First African American Methodist Episcopal Pentecostal & Evangelical Missionary Baptist Church of Charismatic Poets, we'll show you how to make those troubles fade so come ride the waves!

We'll show how to shake off that shag, speak the life you wish you had. We're waiting here to rinse and recondition your roots but you gotta reach out. Don't let life's kinks keep you captive. Come be the person you wish you could be, believe you can be anything through the power of spoken word and poetry.

    Sincerely,
     Pastor Always B. Wright,
     Waiting Here To Change Your Life

This message was paid for by The Weaveangelcial Missionary Coalition

MYSTORY
(mystery)

As I pondered the production of this particular piece about my
people's past I realized I was not up to the task.

In point of fact, I was quite ignorant to the task.
They don't teach my story... just his story,
four hundred freakin' years of his story.
Empires built on my people's back and they get all the glory.

I know we were pimped at the market place and sold like
whores. I know about Malcolm, Martin and Marcus, but there's
got to be more.

Hewey P. ain't new to me.
I know about Mae C. Jemison
and her *Endeavour(s)* on the shuttle.
I know Rosa Parked, on the bus
and watched while white folks fussed and cussed,
but there's got to be something greater about us.

I recall that Carver was clever enough to come up with a
cornucopia, a plethora of purposes for the peanut.
But Jiffy and Peter Pan ain't paying my people in profit or
praise, and I know that back in the days Morgan invented the
stop light and the gas mask, but there's got to be something
deeper in my past.

As my ignorance and desire fought,
I sought deeper historical thoughts.

My yearnings took me to places of higher learning.
The buildings were aged with ivy so they had to have the true
story. But their professor of science thought I was defiant when I
said Edison don't get all the credit,
and there really was no need to debate it.

Because I know the world stays illuminated
'cause Latimer was in the lab when the light was created!
His imagination, intelligence, and diligence created the filament.
So the next knucklehead that says the Negro is lazy –
cut that fool with the truth when they say we can't!
Tell'em Latimer developed the first central electric power plant.
New York, London and Toronto's nights stay bright 'cause he
delivered the electricity for their lights!
Their professor of literature was less than pleased when I
painted this picture...

Once again they steal the glory,
Three white musketeers but a black man wrote the story.
Alexander Dumas is who I present, a light-skin Frenchman of
African descent; their stolen glory; his true story.

And there's no animosity.
I'm just trying to find a place where I can grasp the truth about
my past.

On my journey, I discovered that Hannibal wasn't some cannibal
on the movie screen,
nor was he the leader of the A-Team.
Worst defeat the Romans had ever seen was at the hands of this
African,
and to this day if you look close you'll still find
Hannibal's soldiers in the Italian bloodline.

And I discovered the Emancipation Proclamation was an illegal
piece of documentation. It freed slaves in a land where Lincoln's
law was less than legal.

And I know Jesse Owens ran for the gold,
but when the truth was told,
a black man won the race to the North.
Henson got there first cause Perry's toes got cold.

And to this day his music remains a classical standard —
did you know Beethoven was called the black Spaniard?

And I don't know if this black woman was a professor or a
waitress but the Wachowski brothers stole her manuscript and
re-titled it... "The Matrix!"

Now you would think with all of this,
my people would get a more proportionate portion of American
profit and ownership —
since we did invent the potato chip.

When it comes this particular sect of the human race,
I can talk till I'm black in the face and passed out on the floor.
But when you walk away from this poem,
the only thing you need to remember is:
when it comes to black folks...
there's always more.

MINE

Look at it.
It's an ugly little thing ain't it?

You gave it to me and you can't have it back.

I claim it.

I will hold on to it till I don't want to hold on to it anymore.
It's mine now.

No you can't play with it, don't even look at it.
Let your eyes glaze over with guilt and ignorance when it passes
by you.
Pretend it isn't even there.

Despite all my mamma taught me,
I will never share this one with you.

Truth be told I don't even like it,
most days it makes me sick.

I think I'll let it sit, in the corner,
collect dust,
maybe I'll let it decay and rust,
but YOU...
You will never be allowed to play with it.

I'm the captain of this team
and if you were the only player I had to choose I'd play alone.

Cause when you get it,
when you play with it,
it becomes vile like the venom that dripped from your
grandfathers' fangs.

No matter how far removed you may be from days gone by, even when it's dried & withered there's something about your saliva that reconstitutes all the evil that birthed it.

It's like a Twinkie.
People believe it'll last forever.
How can something manmade last sooo long and still be good for you?
I don't even like Twinkies,
but sometimes I get a taste for it,
but you can't have none.
Cause its mine.

This... this loathsome little thing is mine.

I can make it funny, cute even bonding like super glue.
I can make it even more repugnant than it is, but not you.
It's only poison in your hands with no hope of redemption.

The best way to keep a weapon formed against you from prospering is to take control of it.
Weapon on safe, magazine dropped, chamber cleared.
Sometimes I feel like a werewolf hoarding all the silver bullets.

Far from precious but it's mine.
Like so many it started its existence innocent enough but the inferno of ignorance hatred and greed warped it.
On a good day I could never be proud of this perversion but...
It's mine.

This grotesque offspring of hideous intent is in my hands now. I will be its caretaker. Its future, how it prospers or fails belongs to me.

This... word...

nigga.

Is mine!

39

equal thing.

Res Judicata – "Judged thing."

Respondeat Superior – "Let the superior respond."

Rigor Mortis – "Stiffness of death."

Semper Anticus – "Always forward."

Semper Fidelis – "Always faithful."

Semper Fortis – "Always brave."

Semper Primus – "Always first."

Servian

Sic – "T

Sola Fi

Sola Gr

Sola Sc

Status current

– PART 3 –
VERSUS

"Towards."

Sub Rosa – "under the rose." A thing done secretly or in private.

Tabula Rasa – "Scraped tablet." A blank slate or starting over.

Tempus Fugit – "Time flees." Time is short. Time flies.

Terra Firma – "Solid land." The ground.

Terra Incognita – "Unknown land."

Ultra Vires – "Beyond powers." To do something without authority.

Veni, Vidi, Vici – "I came, I saw, I conquered."

Vera Causa – "True cause."

Verbatim – "Word for word."

Veritas Vos Liberabit – "The truth will set you free."

Versus – "Towards." One side at odds with another.

Veto – "I forbid."

Vox Populi – "Voice of the people."

HAI·KU
俳句

YOU CANNOT STAND THE SMELL OF YOUR
OWN HANDS
CAUSE YOU WON'T LET THAT SHIT GO.

OH HEY!
I ALMOST DIDN'T SEE YOU OVER THERE...
HIDING FROM THE TRUTH

DAMN!
HAVE TO BREAK UP WITH GIRLFRIEND.
CAN'T DO WHITE AFTER LABOR DAY.

(HER RESPONSE)
GUESS I'M SINGLE NOW
I'LL BE FINE
ONLY 60 DAYS TILL BLACK FRIDAY!
~ KBB

YOU GONNA EAT THAT? (PORK YOU)

"Hey my brotha," he began...

Offering me peaces and blessings when what I wanted was to
be left in peace while I was blessing my food.

"Hey my brotha. You not gone eat that pig are you?"
I gently laid down the trident I was using to dive into my sea of
succulent swine, cause if I gripped it too long he might get
forked up.

I didn't want to take all day to traverse all 360 degrees cause if
my dinner dropped more than 2 degrees, I was gonna be
peeved.

I began...
For the purposes of this conversation let's agree that the Bible is
more than metaphors and allegory stories. Let's check the score.

When the man Moses and his flock of fools wandered the desert
for forty 'cause they failed in faith he laid down the law of not
eating pork.

Maybe it's because they couldn't cook and cure it right.
Cause you know pork has to be cooked just right.
Like with mushroom gravy, a little Lawry's,
maybe some sautéed onions.

But God said everything that creepeth and crawleth
is fit for you to eat.
Call nothing I have made unclean
and it's not what goes in a man that defiles him
but what comes out.

Like the garbage that goes in your ears then sung out.
Are you Hip, or did that just Hop over your head?

42

Down your throat isn't the only way you get fed.
Your eyes are the gates to your soul
so what are you putting in your head?

The meat you eat goes in your belly and purged
so don't worry about that shit.
What comes out your mouth comes from that piece of meat
that keeps your beat like a finely tuned metronome
and I gotta tell you...
That jukebox in your temple home is playing sour notes.
Like a tone-deaf jazz band caged behind your ribs.
Mmmmm ribs.
Stop worrying about the pork I chew
and think more about the swine you spew.

Instead of kick-starting conversations about what's on my plate,
right here, let's focus on the atmosphere.
There is infinitely more poison in the air over cities
than in pork
and you ain't stopped breathing that.
Your rhetoric needs to be muffled, it's exhausting.

Do you filter every particulate of filth from the water that
touches your tongue?
You know, my brotha, the water's unclean.
The level of contaminates in our tap is obscene.
It's absorbed through your skin.
Did you shower my friend?

And even more obscene
are the scenes our children have seen on movie screens.
So when I sup over my pork-laced pizza
I'll be damned if I'm gonna let you make me feel like I'm killing
myself,
or a murder defendant on trial...

Cause you know you'd smoke that sausage

if it had nicotine in it.

I know you, my brotha.
I know you weren't worried about the cleanliness of the last
vagina you invaded.
I know you ate it.

My sista,
how come you was cool with that pig you let cum in you?
I bet you wanna blame it on the alcohol.

I've had a few reckless evenings where I may have eaten one
too many honey glazed ham and macaroni & cheese
sandwiches.
But Porky Pig never had me hurting from hangovers or hurling
out my heart while hugging porcelain thrones.
It never made my kids terrified to come home or a danger on
the road.
My blood pork level never made me too sluggish to think,
alter reflexes, run red lights or extinguish a family of four in the
blink of an eye...
I...
Think we should spend more time worrying about the trash we
breathe, the garbage we read, how we water our seeds, and the
things this world needs, than lecturing me about the food my
God gave me to eat.

That's all folks!

EGGS FOR BREAKFAST

When I spread the pages of my favorite poetry book
I only penetrate it's perimeter
with the permanence of a pen's ink drop,
I dare not erase a word or thought,
a mistaken line ejaculated from my Bic,
birthed from that book might be dope 9 months from now.

But when I thumb through the sheets
and spread the pages of my favorite lady
the tool I choose to use is more comparable to a pencil.
A mistaken word left on her loose leaf
seems easy to erase.

I was included
but it wasn't my body
not truly my decision
and unlike the well-meaning people picketing the clinic
I offered no protest.
Like most of them I don't believe in abortion... until I need it.

Physical scars heal but the blade of fear and doubt penetrates
her heart so deep the man who stands behind her can't help
but be wounded too.

If I'm wrong about abortion, Father forgive me.
If I'm right about abortion, Father forgive me.

To the Right Honorable Men of the Legislature:
When preparing yourself for a long day of vaginal legislation
and womb regulation
did your self-righteous ass
have eggs for breakfast?

OPEN LETTER #3 – FAKERY

To the people who rub you the wrong way and you're
not sure why:

Your gut tells you something is wrong.
You don't want to feel this.
You want to flip the switch but your irritation with
them is an intangible itch,
a button you can't quite put your finger on.

You see fabricated emotional fits punctuated with
tears that are counterfeit.
They are imposters with simulated emotions
you don't believe in them.
They are 2Pac's hologram, a fabricated echo of truth.
They are a poorly skilled actor cast in a reality
show scripted by some one with no real life
experience.

You imagine that on a hot Texas day you can see the
fake bubbling up through their pores a mockery of a
real person glistening on their skin.

Maybe their sweat is fake
maybe their pores are pretend
maybe the muscles that move their bones are bogus
maybe the piece of meat in the middle of their torso
that forces air across the vocal chords shaped by
lying lips is only as tangible as freedom.
Maybe the only real thing about them is the
unexplainable discomfort felt when they are in a
room.
No they haven't hurt you, wronged you, or disrespected
you (that we know of).

You just don't like them.

I just, don't like you.

THE STENCH

Upon initial contact with olfactory bulbs,
deceptively sweet particles trigger a response in grey matter
causing nostrils to spread wide recreating prom night 1991.

Then, mere seconds later, the bait and switch.

There's a distinct aromatic undertone that forces primal instinct
to take over.
Body shutters,
nostrils close,
hand over nose,
for emergency back-up
lips clenched to block the stench,
all before my conscious mind realizes
the 1944 Normandy style nasal invasion has begun.

The noisomeness can easily be compared to...
the aroma of infected fecal matter, marinated in rancid milk
after electricity has failed to provide the refrigerator with
adequate fuel to keep the particles under control.

This is akin to the reaction had...
when you start bringing up old shit.

I'm tired of arguing with you.
You don't fight fair.

So I stay on edge,
each potential moment has me poised and ready
for the mental funk I must face waiting for the partially digested
corn, stomach flu after math contents to hit the fan.

Staying on alert to overreact to protect my senses from more of
your bullshit. Flinched, nose clenched, I'm ready.

It smells like you won the argument,
before it even starts.

Strength of will has been sapped from holding breath in
anticipation of the next nasal incursion.
I know a fight's coming,
it's a premonition,
similar to knowing the room's about to smell of fermented
cherries, lactose in-tolerated milk, broccoli and Taco Bell.
I can't tell you how I know,
but the tone in your voice alerts me much the same as bellies
rumbling or butt trumpeting a flatulated flute,
the foreshadow of shit to come.

You know how you continue to smell something even after you
think you're clear of the area?
It's because the particles linger in your nose
a memory of our last epic battle.
Can I wash out yesterday's drama before a new onslaught?

Here's some tissue
and some baby wipes
and some hand sanitizer
and take this Febreeze.

I will help you wash your hands of what's bothering you.

But we gotta let this shit go.

BEAUTIFUL MAN

It moves me to see men do beautiful things while still being
men.
It marvels me to see men move with melodies while still
maintaining their masculinity.
There is strength in your dance,
so don't be afraid to be a man.

It's okay for you to be exactly what God created you to be.
Don't allow the demasculinization of our society make you think
that your penis is any less thing than a blessing.
Don't let the world castrate and cut short the value of the life
that courses and cums up through you... it is not a curse.

Men don't be afraid to be men when expressing you through
the power of verse. It was word that first gave birth to the
universe.

I once heard a boy,
B-YOUNG, man
command the stage and control scene when he spit about
being... a queen.
How if he could be, he would be... a queen.
The piece was powerful,
I was floored
'cause he was talking about being the most powerful piece on
the chessboard.
He honored women while never not being a man.
His words are beautiful.

Seeing men loving men in a manner in which men were meant
to love makes me weep.

Three men, who never really meet, make love through a meal.
Man number three sees man number two scrape to the plate a
portion to a man who more than likely is viewed as less than.

49

Overwhelmed with the gesture man number three buys dinner for the two and for a brief moment the three become one.
It was beautiful.

Beautiful like a man who flat-lines preserving the lifeline of a fallen friend on the frontline is
beautiful like a man who can braid, twist, lock and corn row the crown of his daughters head is beautiful.

Men kiss your baby boy and tell him you love him,
it's beautiful.
Men keep your babies out the street,
it's beautiful.
Honor your woman,
it's beautiful.
Praise your God in public and be beautiful.

I AIN'T NO PUNK! But you're being a BITCH if you think I'm a punk because that man's gesture gives me chills.
Just because you're a man doesn't mean you can't be beauty filled, beauty willed, and beauty skilled.

Man, don't be ashamed if that man's motives makes your forearm follicles do standing ovations.

It's ok to have heart skip beat sensations.

This... is just your body's natural response to God, moving in your midst.

Man let the world see you a stand and be a man.
... It is sooo beautiful!

GODS AND MORTALS

We gods, who reign in the realm of our sheets,
in the kingdom of our beds,
concealed behind the closed doors of our worlds
have no quarrel with you
                              mortals.

You must be mortals 'cause lesser beings always attempt to
escape the reality of their own pathetic existence by pondering
and meddling in the affairs of those greater than them.

You wield pens like swords in an effort to govern us.
As if your laws could dictate the direction our hearts choose to
move.

With all the power at our grasp, even we have little control over
a muscle that sets it's own rhythm.

We can affect the heart but we cannot control it.
You who has the volume of your nose turned up so loud you
can't even hear the rhythm of your own heart.

How dare you stand in judgment of me, you little... Person!

Why are you so concerned with who I sleep with?
It will never be you!

I will no longer stand quiet
as you attempt to judge me with your tiny little mind,
whose grasp is too short-sighted
to even reach the hem of my garment.

This is your issue! You need healing!

So I stand before you closet door open wide...

51

proudly proclaiming...

that I am...
a blanco-sexual.

That's right, I like white women.

Truth be told I go all shades.

There was this blackberry beauty that had me wanting to pawn
my kingdom so I could put a rock the size of Mount Olympus
on her hand. But she only likes white men.

NO MATTER! Because I like Asians, Persians, Hispanics,
Europeans, Africans...
let's just say I have a fetish for homo sapiens.

The color of one's skin and the concentration of their melanin is
of little concern to me.

I like women,
but most importantly,
I like love.

Even if you think my choice ungodly, unnatural or just wrong, it
is my choice and my life to answer for,
on the only day of judgment that matters.

      Brothers,   Sisters,   Mortals,
this matter of my heart is not an issue that warrants the kindling
of disdain that sears yours.

You too will stand before the throne of judgment and answer
for the blackened scorch marks burned in your heart,
from an ungodly hatred that was not your cause to carry.

a life and deeds.

De Facto – "By Deed."

Deus Ex Machina – "God from the machine."

Dramatis Personæ – "The parts of the play." Characters in a drama.

E Pluribus Unum – "Out of many, one."

Editio Princeps – "First edition." The first printed edition of a work.

Emeritus – "Veteran." The position held at the point of retirement, as an honor.

Ergo – "Therefore."

Et Al – "And others."

Et Cetera – "And the rest." And so on.

Ex Gratia – forming an act

Ex Post ward." A law w

Fiat L

Fortes

Gloria in Excelsis Deo – "Glory to God in the Highest."

Habeas Corpus – "You have the body."

In Absentia – "In the absence."

In Situ – "In the place." In the original place or appropriate position.

In Vitro – "In glass."

In Vivo – "In a living thing."

Ipso Facto – "By the fact itself."

Magna Cum Laude – "With great praise."

Magnum Opus – "Great work." The masterpiece of an artist's career.

Malum in Se – "Bad in itself." A thing that is inherently wrong.

Malum Prohibitum – "Bad by prohibition." A thing that is only wrong because it is illegal.

Mater Dei – "Mother of God." Mary, who gave

– PART 4 –
EMERITUS
"Veteran."

HAI·KU
俳句

SOLDIERS DO NOT LEAVE THE BATTLEFIELD.
THEY CARRY IT HOME
ON THEIR BACKS.

WE HUMANS

We humans,
naturally drawn to disaster like its dictated in our DNA,
that day, the cacophony of concern that cascaded from the
crowd alerted me to a derailed train of a man.

He laid there, as if run aground,
reminiscent of the Exxon Valdez,
a broken vessel, life oozing away like an Alaskan oil slick.

I, the coast guard cutter siren called by life leaving its shell.

Like New York city, the pulse never sleeps, so there must have
been an accident proximal to his radial cause I felt nothing
when attempting to ascertain the rhythm of his street.

As if pulled over by a profiling patrolmen,
his heart... arrested.

I wonder if calamity cared about his color.
Did death know he was black?

His daughter will say "I never met him."

Fellow soldiers say Specialist Marquise Mobley,
was a tower, but the way he collapsed couldn't have been fist
punched airplane attacks his body imploded straight down like
controlled demolition,
it had to be an inside job.

A lifetime of life-saving lessons
lead to my lips being air-locked on his,
      desperately,
         hoping I could diaphragm squeeze a rejection letter,
            breath stamped,
               addressed to death by way of his lungs,

delivery hastened with heart pounding,
mine in my chest,
my hands pounding on his.

Death got the message and responded with a loudly silent...

...from the man I was saving.

That exhale was the last thing I heard Marquise say.

We mortals think ourselves gods,
attempting to put spilled milk back into fractured containers.

Then take it personal when we can't fix what we didn't break...

or make.

3 STRAWS

I am the camel's back
                3 straws beyond its breaking point,
attempting to speak my silence into spoken word.

I have a scar,
the aftermath of wounds.
X marks the spot, the treasure being the knowledge that your
body beat back the invader but, what do you do when you can't
see the wound or find the scar?

Not all wounds can be cared for by the loving adhesive
embrace of a Band-Aid,
the military doesn't break everyone
but it usually leaves a scar...
somewhere.

We soldiers,
we sacrifice our civil rights like,
freedom of speech and doing as we please,
we all have our personal reasons.
The irony is we do it dying, fighting for your freedoms.
In exchange we gain goods and opportunities
but neither the recruiter nor the contract conveyed the
complexity of the price we would pay.
Now I'm trying to raise my voice above a whisper
but unable to yell pass the pain of unidentified anguish.

Politicians may pull us puppets from the theater of their war but
the battles in our soul wages on,
fighting concepts like survivor's guilt – an oxymoron.
Some of us drink to drown the damage we cannot find,
we fill the emptiness with smoke coke and wine,
trying to silence the subtle siren of fallen friends,
our sanity the new front line.

We are grenades,
                    ready
                to
                    explode.

We come home still doing what we were trained to do. Locked,
loaded,
sometimes family gets caught in the cross hairs.
We are not monsters.
                    We are mortars
                            landmines
                                the well-trained M16,
somebody forgot to remove my firing pin.

Some of us escape the job of living,
painting our own pink slips at the point of bullets revolved,
chambered and swallowed cause it's got to be better than the
pills the V.A.[1] pushes, unable to push past the pain.
War always leaves a stain and not all of us can sustain past the
imperceptible pain.
I wanna talk but it hurts.

I ain't no punk.
It's not that easy to man up.
I ain't scared it hurts,
physically,
like fist gripped sternum,
cardiac clutched,
crushed if I dare to conversate what I've seen.

It's like my pain is classified
and no one has clearance.
If I dare to speak,
anxiety attacks like snipers and IED's,[2]
I wanna talk but it hurts.

I wonder what would happen if drive my car into that tree.

                                        Would it hurt?

So we eat pills
              or shotguns,
because the memories we swallowed have soured our
stomachs.

Celexa and Prozac protect me like
seatbelts, Kevlar and blankets,
restraining me,
making me untouchable,
and it feels good in here.
I like not giving a damn.

It bothers me that I don't give a damn,
but I don't really give a damn,
cause without it,
I am the camel's back
                3 straws beyond my breaking point.

So I keep the carnage chemically contained cause if I don't
bottle the pain it'll spill,
all over those I love,
and unlike them...
                I signed up for this shit.

1. V.A. - Veteran's Administration
2. IED - Improvised Explosive Devise

59

BARE NAKED CITY

There is understandable confusion when speculating on the
origin of the monster, "Godzilla."
Was it awakened by atomic testing?
Was it created by the test?
Or were the tests simply covering up an attempt to destroy it?

This is my truth.

It slumbered for so long,
quiet and bothering no one.
Choked into silence by the passage of time.
Laid away by a world that didn't need it
and refused to support it
but some things don't die,
they just sleep.

Like the pain of friends dying too young.
Like the memories of fellow soldiers reduced to convenient
sandwich sized pieces.
Memories can be monsters.

Triggered by an explosive event of immeasurable hurt/power.
A monstrous pain,
a strange creature, Kaiju, rose from the deep.

Monsters like this are too big to strike without warning.
Even if blind to the signs there's always advance notice.
Shaking ground, shaky hands and shifting tides.
I try to hide the rising tide of salt water leaking from my face.

Crying is an outward manifestation of an
overwhelming emotional event

If only these tears were enough to extinguish the fires that will
be left behind from the next rampage.
If only rising waters threatening to drown me
were just rising waters threatening to drown me.
But these rising waters sweltering in my eyes only signify what's
to come, what keeps coming back.

This force of nature, a neutral evil that could care less how it
destroys me.

I rebuild,
it returns,
I rebuild, it returns.

I am depressed by the weight of these memories/monsters.
Even men get stuck in the depression of its footprints,
this monster only destroys.
It's just hard to hear us yelling for help
'cause these holes are so deep.

My heart is a bare-naked city.
Armed with years of experience
but virtually defenseless
against this Kaiju formed of ghostly memories.
This Gojira of pain seems unstoppable.
It is stomping through every defense I have erected.
The horror is not the sheer size of it
but my complete inability to fight back.

LET'S HAVE A WAR

A poet named Buddy Wakefield once asked me if I believe what
he believes.
If I didn't he would invite me and my family over
so his family and my family could have a war...
cause that's what we do.

FIGHT!

I don't know about your god,
but my God has to be better than yours.
Why else would I follow him?
It has nothing to do with my mama making me,
although I know most of you got YOUR beliefs that way.

My God makes beautiful things to roam and decorate the land.
Turns them into food that turns into shit that feeds the flowers
that turn into food to make the beautiful things that roam and
decorate the land.
Can yours do that?

Mine ignites the horizon
with sunrises and sunsets like life and death.
He waters the world with much needed rains and still
apologizes by painting the skies with bows.

My God hung the crescent moon Allahu Akbar.
He poked a hole in the universe and called it the Star of David.
Shalom.
My God crossed out His own Son just to open a door
I was unworthy to walk through.
Hallelujah.
My god, MY GOD!

What I believe in is what's right
and anyone who disagrees will get left or dealt with.

It's not that my God doesn't want me to kill my fellow man,
he doesn't want me to murder, unjustly take a life.
So we've been known to kill
anyone who doesn't believe in him the way we believe in him,
even if it means they die
before they get a chance to see his light shining in us.

Maybe if God had shined bright enough on them
then I wouldn't have been able to see how wrong they truly are.

He's got more names than man can imagine
and they're all worth killing in.

Call it crusades, inquisitions or democracy.
The lifeless rocks we fight for beneath our feet are worth it.
Our fights are holy,
there's nothing like a good old fashioned jihad.
Let's have a war!

How dare you be a witch,
or a nigga,
or a faggot,
or a woman out of place
or poor white trash
I dare you to be different!

My God is bigger than yours.
I know because I measured
and even though I have yet to reach the end of his width, depth
or breath and love,
                            (and Love?)
I know he's bigger than yours.
                            (and Love?)

Hold on!
What if my God is so big
that my God IS your God?

63

It's different and the same
and exactly what we both need at the same time.

So un-understandably so,
our God is bigger
and more encompassing
than we could possibly imagine.
Down-sized into bits and pieces so we ants can fit it in the
narrow passages of our understanding it individually in the best
way we are capable of.

The Minbari$_1$ believe that the universe is sentient
and it breaks off pieces of itself to explore itself to get a better
understanding of itself.

I like being a piece of the universe.
I think even science can agree with this definition.

So Mr. Wakefield,
if you believe God created us all,
loves us all,
and looks forward to us coming home to him/her/it one day,
then I think we all believe the same thing.

1 See Babylon 5 by J. Michael Straczynski

Carpe Diem – "Seize the Day."
Christus Rex – "Christ the King."
Cogito Ergo Sum – "I think therefore I am."
Consensu – "With consent."
Corpus Christi – "Body of Christ."
Cum Laude – "With praise."
Cura Personalis – "Care for the whole person."
Curriculum Vitae – "Course of life." Overview of
a life and deeds.
De Facto – "By Deed."
Deus Ex Machina – "God from the machine."
Dramatis Personæ – "The parts of the play."
Charac~~ters in a drama~~

– PART 5 –
CONSENSU
"With consent."

E Pluri~~
**Editio~~
printed~~
**Emerit~~   the
point o~~
Ergo –~~
Et Al – "And others."
Et Cetera – "And the rest." And so on.
Ex Gratia – "From grace." Voluntarily performing
an act purely out of kindness,
Ex Post Facto – "From a thing done afterward."
A law with retroactive effect.
Fiat Lux – "Let there be light."
Fortes in Fide – "Strong in faith."
Gloria in Excelsis Deo – "Glory to God in the
Highest."
Habeas Corpus – "You have the body."
In Absentia – "In the absence."
In Situ – "In the place." In the original place or
appropriate position.
In Vitro – "In glass."
In Vivo – "In a living thing."

HAI·KU
俳句

PART TIME COSMETOLOGIST AND BOXER.
SPENDS NIGHTS BOBBING,
DAYS WEAVING.

SOMETHING I'VE NOTICED
THAT AS MY BEARD GETS WHITER
I GET MORE PRIVILEGE

OPPOSED TO
GENETICALLY ALTERED FOOD.
TILL I TASTED A CUTIE.

HER HAIR

She moves with a sway that'll fishhook your eyes.

She's a sunlit sundial with clockwork hips,
    she moonwalks,
        she space walks,
            she shows off
                she does everything
            but actually walk.
            She floats,
                she glides,
                    she waterfalls,
        she mermaids in moonlight.

Translation: I find her to be somewhat attractive.

She's more Moor than European by the way of some island,
but today her perfectly mixed breed hair halted my normal
testosteroned gaze.
                    Freshly done,
        front stoop, corn rows table spooned her head
      with five dollar weave struggling to grip "good hair."

Had me wondering if her collage of genetic heritage made it
hard for her to grip one culture or the other
like Teflon laced hair Hawaiian silky track glue won't stick to.

She's ivory shoe laced, black Chucks, reflecting the color of clay
              not knowing what circle is safe to walk in,
                    maybe that's why she floats.

          Her hair don't confederate flag in the wind.
    It don't lock like ebony arms protesting for civil rights,
    it don't ball up like fingers and fists on a border fence.
      It snakes in the humidity, it curly fries when wet.

You can't just spoon out each individual ingredient in the stew that makes you. So why do we see the amalgamation of genetic pot-lucked perfection and try to grab whatever strand we can claim is like we?

Weave don't last long.
She shares the struggle of her hair,
trying to hold onto something identifiable
but this fake shit won't stick.

When I say fake shit,
that's actually a metaphor for the people who smile in your face
but hate that they can't see a semblance of their own reflection.

Arrogance demands to be fueled
by seeing your own face everywhere you look.
When familiar features are found or unfound they'll Willie A
Lynch pin to hook on you their trailer of stereotypes and
imposed expectations.

Are we teaching this ugly or birthing it?
'Cause, even children hatefully pull real hair looking for Jerri
curls, weaves and extinctions like it's some "Imitation of Life".
This is a desire for culture, for roots that hold firm.

She is working on keeping her heritage straight not her hair.
She'll never be white enough.
If she can native her tongue she'll have a slim chance of being
Hispanic enough.

Catch her on the evening news she's got a good chance of
being black enough.

Her acceptance will come on the day
we decide to be human enough.

DEAR BEARD

I have a great deal of love,
                respect,
                            and admiration for,
 my beard.

He punctuates my profile,
he distinguishes me,
I'm happy every day I wake up and he's still there.
He doesn't get in the way of kisses but he's always close
enough to catch crumbs so they don't dive bomb the floor.
He's considerate like that.

True story:
I didn't go back to the Army,
cause I couldn't part with my beard.
We became friends when I was 15,
before he was fully developed and either of us truly knew how
to define the other.
I remember when the first coarsely curled hair reached through
the skin of my chin
like a seedling determined to be a mighty oak.
Despite how short and black he was
I noticed him.

Since then, we've had an on and off and on again love affair,
mostly off
because the military had an issue with our relationship.
Even when hiding him,
he always manages to shadow me,
he's punctual like 5 o'clock.

But lately, I've wanted to erase the monochrome collage of
color that loiters below my lips.
I've bought hair dye,
imagined washing my jaw in bootblack,

and I dream of taking Sharpie to each individual curl.

Some of our friends started calling him "sellout."
I often wonder if he gets more noticed now for his whiteness,
or does he seek attention by being whiter.

I asked my beard why it sees fit to betray me.
Why did it feel the need to Michael Jackson its way away from
the black bristle majesty that cushions my chin?
Are you ashamed of our ebony?
Are you protesting the label of Black, or African American?
Is this your way of saying you just want to be, American?

Dear Beard,

If you have problems with labels,
then why do you allow me to label you, "Beard?"

You don't have a problem with the designer labels
on the shampoos and conditioners you demand.
You want all the name brand combs and clippers,
those all have labels!

I suspect you have a problem with labels because you're
ashamed of your roots.

No matter how mixed you may be, beard, you're still black.
Nobody cares that our last name is Brown.
Nobody cares that it's the name of our Irish ancestors
and not our ancestor's owners.
Nobody cares that we can trace our roots to Africa and Ireland.
When people see you they won't see the white,
at best they'll call you grey but under their breath,
behind their doors, you'll still be black.
Black can be a burdensome thing, a weight, maybe,
maybe, Beard,
you're getting too old to hold on to it.

He responded:

Dear Face, *(I love that he calls me face).*

Calm, down.
This is not about color or culture.
You misunderstand my intent.

I am only labeling our moments in this world.
These platinum strands are what distinguish you.
They separate you from those who have no proof of trial and
survival.
Each tuft is a testament.

Dying me would be killing every silver lining I saved from
our cloudy days!

I will not let you
boot black me into a shameful kind of black face.
I would die before I let you dye me!

Face, there is no shame in this contrast.
This is something we've created together.

Forever yours,
Beard

ZOMBIE LOVE

As if trying to consume my very essence,
maybe trying to understand my presence,
she keeps picking at my brain.
Her and I are not the same.
I thought I was sane but she keeps driving me in... love.

More compatible than I could comprehend
'cause she wants to feast on my dead decaying heart
like some sorta vulture.
I wanna give it to her
but love like this can be torture.

So I gave her unchecked control of my cardiac
convinced she would keep it in good care.
I had no conception she would consume it along with all the
love I had to give.
It scares me
the way I love how she savors every piece of me that I offer her,
I think I'm losing myself.

How long can I survive this kind of love?
The more I give her, the more of me she wants
she's picking at me piece by piece.
I know she loves me, she must 'cause she wants all of me
and frankly I'm dying to be with her.

I don't wanna live beyond this love.
I offer my feet on her alter,
no need to kick it with my boys anymore.
I gave her my right leg so she knows at the end of each day I
won't be walking away with what's left.

No need for knees
I gladly give her these
forget kneeling!

73

The way I'm feeling
I lay my love, life and body before her.

She is the only one for me hands down,
hands off
I offer her my hand,
it's hers and now she knows it will never be raised against her.

If you see her
don't let her lack of an ostensible smile,
make you think she is anything other than happy.
The aftermath of cancer causes my core to run warmer than
normal so I take no notice to how cold she can be.

Outsiders wonder why I find her so drop dead gorgeous,
a dead ringer,
got my love dead to rights.
Life without her?
Fate worse than death.
The way we love is dead on point.

I tell them, with this kind of love you don't even have to try.
We love so hard "till death do us part", don't even apply.

What we have quite literally, biochemically is an impossibility.
Religiously our love is heresy.

From night, to dawn, to day.

She's my Zombie love and I'm happy this way.

DRINK

I love the way she melts in my arms,
spills into my hands so I drink.
Drink like my life depends on getting as much of her in me as
possible. We be the perfect metaphor for infinity. Her in me and
me in her and we be one.
Like the one puddle she leaves in my mattress
a reflecting pool so I reflect.

                              Like the reflection she leaves in my eyes
                                   a blinding light burns brilliant
                                   her beautiful frame to my brain.
Then a touch,
A kiss and we can't resist the kiss.

                         Imagine this,
            silk satin and cashmere warm melting on your mouth.
          Tongues dance to the drums of a smooth heart beat rhythm.
               Arms wrapped round waist pulling breast to chest.
                    Left hand caresses back
                like I was playing bass in an all skin band
                   while neck rests in right hand.

So enamored we touch fingers to face and lips just to convince
     the rest of the body we are actually enjoying something as
                         much as this beautifully simple kiss.

               I nuzzle neck and pause
            to feel her life pulse pass my lips.
Palms pay alms to arms to position her right where I need her.
    I delicately un-wrap my favorite piece of candy
         mouth-watering wet, I'm ready to eat.

                         I deep sea dive into her,
            legs wrapped round my head like scuba gear.

75

Lips meet lips between hips locked
like she's my only source of oxygen
I begin.
I shift tongue through lips slow like tectonic plates
until her mountains rise and her earth quakes,
thighs tremble and shake
she tastes,
like a fresh rain waterfall
and I'm The Little Dutch Boy just trying to plug the hole.

The gravity of her situation has forced the tic-tocs of her clock
to slow to forever.
She looks down at me,
sleepy eyed and weary from the long journey.

Soft lips curl back in satisfaction
her eyes almost disappointed I didn't travel with her.
I say; "It's cool. I'll cum next time."

Cause she's standing on the edge and I'm ready to push her off!
Another shift of tongue and lips shakes her concentration.

Her head juts back in an amazing, agonizing kind of awesome
as she desperately fights the tidal wave that erupts from the
explosion she's trying to hide.
Paralyzed with pleasure she can only fantasize about pushing
me away. Praying she can find my off switch before the joy
kills her.

Unable to fight the wave the damn breaks and she spills!
She spills into my hands and I drink her sweet godly nectar.
Thunder rolls in the background Zeus angry that I dared to
drink what used to be his.

I drink like my life depends on getting as much of her in me as
possible. We be the perfect metaphor for infinity.
Her in me and me in her and we were one.

76

ARTHUR

Ladies!
Camelot is a fantasy and the greatness of King Arthur has been
completely over exaggerated.
Sweetened, swallowed and regurgitated.

You may be willing to swallow the truth,
but you'd rather taste the dream.
If you chew a fantasy too long,
eventually lies will get stuck in your teeth and decay
and if you go even one day without rinsing your mouth and
spitting out death,
the next man might not be able to love you past your breath.

When you think about it, how could Guinevere not love a man
like Arthur?
He's handsome, strong, rich... a knight in shiny armor.
He has the power and the means to ensure no one will ever
harm her.
But he doesn't have the wealth to protect her from himself.

So ladies, while you're praying to your fairly odd mother to be
saved by a knight, there's something know.
They always feel the need to rescue someone so...
Once he thinks you're safe, Arthur continues his rescue race
refusing to resist the next sundress in distress.

He seems to care more about the occasional lady in the lake
than the woman by his side.
Ignoring her tear filled eyes, he buys his public respect with
bullion pressed from her neglect.
More worried about chivalry than the caliber of his sword,
Arthur creates another ex.
How many times has Lifetime told tales of rape and abuse,
but what about plain old neglect?
What about her credit? Her respect?

77

Arthur has the finances to fund crusade after crusade
but when it's time to pay attention,
Guinevere too often goes unpaid.

In the face of overwhelming odds Arthur can rally the troops
with a godlike determination.
But when it comes to Guinn he gets an "F" in communication,
as if he just says "F" the communication.

Could it be the shiny armor?
It is shiny.
It does look good.
And all the ladies in waiting love it
when men are sitting high on a horse.

Of course, it's easy to see why a man would wear armor when
he's been burned by a dragon.
What's more, according to the brochure
it also protects him from things like blades, arrows, a monster
wielding a mace (thus the need for the shielded face) and... love.

Yes!
The armor protects him from love.
He might be shielded from a monster with a mace
but when wearing armor
it's hard to see what's right in front of your face.

As rich as he is,
emotional maintenance is not in his budget.
The armor stays shiny cause he won't let anyone touch it.

Armor...
requires as much effort to put on as it does to take off.
So many a nights are spent in bed fully dressed,
at home, alone.

But it's O.K..
Arthur has yet another crusade
and come dawn...
he won't wanna waste time putting any of that shit back on...

Sidebar:
Hmm? Just a thought.
What if I'm mistaken in my summation of the situation?
Maybe Arthur is ashamed of his flame.
Maybe... the peasants are picking on poor Arthur
cause old Guinn's not from Camelot.
Paranoid that his knights are sitting round the table
stirring mess 'cause he's with a woman from Lyonesse.

No matter!

Cause there's one man who doesn't give a damn about horses
and shiny armor, crusades or parades, ladies of the lake and
whether or not his woman is from Camelot.

Guinevere has her eyes on Lancelot.

appropriate position.

In Vitro – "In glass."

In Vivo – "In a living thing."

Ipso Facto – "By the fact itself."

Magna Cum Laude – "With great praise."

Magnum Opus – "Great work." The masterpiece of an artist's career.

Malum in Se – "Bad in itself." A thing that is

– PART 6 –
PERSONA NON GRATA
"Person not pleasing."

Modus Operandi – "Method of operating."

Mutatis Mutandis – "After changing what needed to be changed."

Non Sequitur – "It does not follow." A thing that is absurd because it is out of context

Omnia Vincit Amor – "Love conquers all."

Opus Dei – "The Work of God."

Para Bellum – "Prepare for war."

Pater Familias – "Father of the family."

Pax Americana – "American Peace" The sphere of US influence.

Per Capita – "By heads." Per person.

Per Diem – "By day."

Per Os – "Through the mouth."

Per Rectum – "Through the rectum."

Per Se – "Through itself."

Persona Non Grata – "Person not pleasing." An unwelcome or undesirable person.

Pro Bono – "For good."

Pro Forma – "For form."

Pro Patria – "For country."

HAI·KU
俳句

HIS TONGUE FLIPPED LIKE A QUARTER
DROPPED INTO HER WISHING WELL
HEAD
GETS TAIL.

WHAT IF BULLETS
HAD A UNION
TO PROTECT THEM FROM BEING FIRED

TIGHTEN GUN LAWS
HOMICIDES WOULDN'T DECREASE THE MOST
SUICIDES WOULD

~ JACOB DODSON

NATIONAL HAIKU
DEATH MATCH
CHAMPION
2012

CALIFORNIA KING

Allow me to introduce myself.
I am crafted from the finest pieces of cherry wood,
solid, hard, strong (just how she likes it)
and not that pressed particle board mess with red paint either.
I'm soft, comfortable I keep her cuddled over my springs.

I am a California King (sized bed).
My headboard is padded with the finest Corinthian leather.
My posts rise up toward vaulted ceilings like bald fists at the '68
Olympics and I belong to her.
She's got a name,
but to me she is "Her" cause there is no other she, but her.

She often drapes me in Egyptian Cotton and sheets with
unbelievable thread counts that don't come close to adding up
to how good her skin feels on me.
Curse these springs!
I wish I was a Craftmatic Adjustable
so I could rise up and salute her like... he does.

He!
He has a name but I call him "He" cause I don't rightly give a
damn what his name is.
He's not even a real man,
more like magician the way he folds her into position,
it's gotta be an illusion.
Onetime I heard he tell her that he was an artist attempting to
sculpt the perfect orgasm.
I thought that line was lame,
she just responded,
                    aaahhh...
                              then came.
Last night he walked into the THE BED's ROOM just as she was
warming up my sheets nestled in that in between haze,
she drifting off to a world where her and me could be we.

He pulls off my sheets, all fifteen hundred threads per square inch. Gently drags her to my edge and kneels before her.
Sometimes I can't tell if he's drinking from her wishing well or praying over the bounty he's been blessed with.
Either way she awakes serenading us, HIM, with a song that sounds like impending satisfaction.
He flips his tongue like a silver dollar dropping it in her fountain.
I don't know what he wishes for but it always comes up head and tails.
Smooth move dude! 9.2!

He slides her back on to me then climbs on top of us.
First their eyes connect then lips, then their bodies.
They interlock like the boxcars on a freight train, firm, strong, secure.
He begins his slow build up like the coupling rods on a steam engine.
First the slow push as wheels spin her beautiful moans are the coal that feeds his fire.
The buildup was slow but by the looks of things his smoke stack didn't have long before it would blow.

My favorite part...
I mean the part I freaking hate...
is when he flips her over like freshly fried flapjack,
his form is flawless. 9.5!
And every time she'd whisper,
                    wow
like it's the first time he's ever done it,
as if she wonders how,
eternally impressed that he manages to muscle her delicate frame into a new position.

The souls of her feet lifted high in praise.

Knees drawn back to whisper encouragements and
congratulations in her ear,
'cause the orgasm hurt soo good.
Then 10!
I'm not sure if it was me, or the earth
but one of us shook...

The lamp laughed out loud.
                    Light that ass up, Larry!

The ceiling fan was too cool to comment.

The dresser dialogued,
                    Dig deep, dawg!

The Teddy Bear noticed the lack of latex
                    Pull out playa... Pull ooouut!

No... Oh... She bit my pillow.
                    TEN!!

He quietly rolls off me and exits to the bathroom
and I hear the most beautifully high pitched squeal.
The shower doesn't like his magically artistic bitch ass either.

He's like all the other he's,
came and went.
Now she is left with me, wrapped warmly in my sheets,
appreciated once more.

I'm strong the way she needs me to be.
I'm soft the way she wants me to be.
I... am... her California King.

DARTH-FATHER

Son, you were born to walk the sky,
a life of privilege,
heir to an empire.

I would have given my right hand to walk in your shoes.

You whiney ungrateful bastard,
I would have gladly taken an evil father over no father at all,
a life longing for a man strong in anything just to teach me the
ways of something.

Here I am,
right here reaching out to you,
the key to your past wanting nothing more than for you to rule
the galaxy by my side,
instinctually filled with pride,
father and son, falling in love with you before first sight.

Search your feelings you know it to be true.
The force is strong with you.

Your destiny lies with me Skywalker
but I find your lack of faith disturbing.

Maybe...
you would be more accepting if I hadn't been tainted with the
moniker of "The Dark Side".
Would you have been more understanding if I had been
seduced by:
 – "the misunderstood" side,

– or the "not able to have dad in the home and still collect
welfare" side,

– or the "off fighting for his country, can't be home with you" side,

– or the "incarcerated by a racially biased judicial system" side,

– or the "like a politically corrupt state agency the Jedi plain old lied to your dad and told him you were dead cause they thought they knew what was better for you than your father did side."

    <inhale>

        <exhale>

            <inhale>

                <exhale>

It's a shame
losing my hand didn't keep my curse from touching you.

You were the death of every father figure in your life like,
modern media reflecting the perpetual absence of dad at home.
You got old uncle Owen killed,
Obi Wan dies saving your punk ass,
you abandoned poor Yoda
only to pursue the father you rejected
and you finally accepted my love...
As I'm dying.

Arguably I made a few mistakes;
I got caught up with the wrong crowd,
brought down a republic,
committed genocide,
but to save the life of my wife and child,
you... *(there is another. A girl, your thoughts betray you.)*
My most epic error in judgment
was falling prey to the selfish demented desires of my own father figure,
maybe I would have done better if my dad was around.

I did the wrong things for the right reasons.

I loved your mom, but with a passion that clouded my vision.
If I had known people and life were like sand
I wouldn't have held her beautiful neck so tight.

She slipped so loudly between my fingers my own labored
breath mocks that moment like a bad loop.

<inhale>

<exhale>

Luke,
I'm sorry.
No more excuses.

I was just wrong.

These aren't Death Stars son,
I'm building moons that remind me of your mother's eyes.
The disappointment in them destroyed my whole world.

Son, promise...
you'll be better than me...

change your destiny.

87

CRACKHEAD POET

I started doing poetry in college. My roommate said it would open my mind and expand my knowledge.

Before long it became a social thing, the in-thing
and I was just trying to be down with the scene.
I started going to these private poetry parties with everybody pushing their books and CD's.
I dabbled in some metaphors, alliteration and rhyme you know all the cool kids was doing it at the time.
Then I even tried some of that hard stuff you know that free verse but spoken word was my curse.

At first I'd do a poem, you know,
just something to relax to.
Now I can't get out of bed and make it to breakfast without doing at least two!

I'm fiending for poetry
like Craig and Smokey lookin' for a dime bag.
I just wanna roll my pages like Zig Zag and light it
with lines that flow hot like lava,
making the average poet sweat and slobba'.
I wanna write those pages that ignite stages,
I want those monstrous metaphoric rhymes that's got to be kept behind cages.

After a while I just got so desperate for poetry I put aside that homophobia crap and found myself sitting on some white man's lap...
First time it happens I take a deep breath and pause...
Oh please, please Mr. Claus I swear I'll be good this time.
Just bring me a big ole bag of rhymes.
For for Kwanza just bring me 7 new verses.
I'll pay my tithes if it'll stop *Writer's Block* curses.

I even started muggin' old ladies cause I thought they had
verses in they purses, and what's worse is,
last Easter my wife found me in some kind of poetic haze.
I had hid behind the couch for two whole days...
waitin' for that bunny!
I heard that the Easter bunny and his basket of eggs was
actually a metaphor for life and new beginnings.
I figured a six-foot fluffy-ass metaphor would have some to
spare... I know he ain't real but I ain't care,
when you're fiendin' for poetry you'll get that shit anywhere.

I was messin' with this street poet one time,
just lookin' for some cheap rhymes.
That's when the ink started to drip from my pen...
I had to get treated for a bad case of similes friend.
That's when I learned to keep the cap on my pen.
I knew poetry had become a curse when I sold two kidneys for
just one verse.
Naw... they wasn't my kidneys. Let's just say... I found them.

Thus far, I've lost my house and my car,
so my thumb is how I roam,
hoping I can win some cash at the slam so I can catch the bus
back home. There was a time in my life when I had to be treated
at a mental wellness facility for my attempt to enhance my
ability and poetically spiritual game by injecting ink directly into
my veins... That just caused a lot of pain.

I've paid an ugly price for poetry, I lost my wife for poetry,
I almost lost my life for poetry. Hell, I'll take your life poetry! Cut
me with a knife I'll bleed poetry, I breath poetry,
my weed is poetry. The down fall of man ain't greed... it's
poetry.

Yo man... I'll wash your windows if you'll just let me read some
poetry.

MR. BULLET TAKES A HOLIDAY

I'm here, dressed, standing next in line
but I'm not working
today is a holiday.

I'm fasting from the taste of flesh.
    I will meditate in this chamber.
      I will pray for a better path.
        I might be known for firing off
        but I refuse to spiral out,
          no ricochets,
          no punching holes in walls for me today.

So no matter how hard you squeeze,
        you won't trigger me.
    If the hammer falls it will be in vain.
I will not get innocent blood on my full metal jacket tearing
      through anyone's school today.

    This would be a good time for you to take me back home
      and find a better way to deal with this bully.

Don't be the coward they accuse you of
by getting me to do your dirty work.
Courage is not extinguishing a life
  anybody can do that.
Courage is standing strong when fear threatens to pistol grip
your soul and squeeze an explosion out of you.

Say no,
    say stop,
        ask for help.

Have you bothered telling the teacher, your parents
or just punching that bastard in his mouth?

Excuse me Sir.

> Feeling down is not a good reason to pick me up,
> so put me down.

The only thing you're going to get today is a tired hand
and a wet barrel,
'cause I refuse to cavatate my way through the cavity of your
skull.

I will not Glock you out of your misery!
I will not be your after dinner mint or midnight snack!
I will not be your retirement package or your pathway to peace!
I will not be the last thing on your mind today!

What if I told you the voices of guilt would follow you to the
next world and my "click, click boom" will not drown them out?

I'm giving you the day to find something to be happy about,
like the perfect number of holes you already have in your head.
You're beautiful,
> you're valuable,
> > someone loves you,
> I forgive you,
> > I gift you more time to figure it out.

> > > Mister Officer,
> > > I've been scoping the situation
> > and from my point of view your life is not in danger.
> > > I will not justify this homicide,
> > I will not help you fill in that pre-drawn chalk outline
> > > no one is dying to see it.
> I will not be the exclamation point for your irrational fear,
> > prejudice, ignorance or just plain stupidity.
> > > Yes, I'm questioning your caliber.
> > > You need more training.
> > > Your instincts stink.

91

That's an old man with a cell phone.
That's a young man speeding to his wedding.
That's a little boy, peddling weed to feed his momma.
Do black people remind you of the shadows that haunt you?

Here's a suggestion,
take off your badge and throw that at him.
It's not like you know how to use it.

Haiku Interlude:

Killer cops leaving a bad taste in your mouth?
Well then,
Try indict-mints!

Dear soldier,
your mission has been canceled today!

No ma'am,
I will not break into pieces in your husband's heart
because he broke yours!

I'm sorry you got cut off,
but I'm not your I35 or L.A. highway revenge.

I will not plunge myself into the back of that child
for stealing gum, cigarettes and Chico Sticks!

You will not use me to coerce anyone out of a fresh pair of kicks
or drugs.

There will be no accidents cause I won't budge.
NOT TODAY!

...I am not protesting our 2nd amendment

92

but exercising my 1st.

I hope the silence of this hollow point makes the point.
I will not be anyone's assassin today...

Mr. Bullet...
Is taking a holiday.

JOB
אִיּוֹב

Job hears a still quiet voice from behind.

Get your hands in the air.

Job reaches for the sky,
high as if he had hope hidden in a cloud.

With a thump out loud his heart squeezes harder to hurl to his
out stretched limbs a little extra life.
His autonomic response unaware in this situation,
he can neither flee nor fight.

In the time it takes to blink he thinks and time seems to slow to
a standstill, as many of his most memorable moments move
past his eye like blue ray.
No promises have been made this might be his last day.

Make no mistake; Job's love of life is not fake.
Happiness and prosperity follow him like a big-eared puppy
begging to play as if fortune was genetic like someone born
that way.

But the memories that haunt him are of the hearts he broke.

The bitter memory he's given to others makes him choke like a
gallon of bitter tears forced down his throat.

He mourns the seeds he carelessly planted with wild ways.
The flowers he uprooted in his younger days
and the beauty of blossoms that will never bloom
'cause he was too selfish to raise.

He remembers those he tortured with his untamed tongue.

Gossip like a stake...

in the heart of those he hates for hates sake
and trailing all that, is the shadow of his many mistakes.
But then... he remembers how blessed he's been, from his last
breath to the next one. His son's... Two beautiful boys his
personal success and spiritual treasures AND his unending joy.
Jostled, Job, jets out his mouth,

Just a minute. I know that voice. Who are you?

One of his capturers replies,

I AM

I AM... who?

**I am Him, Horis, Jah, Jehovah, The Great One, The
Morning Sun, the beginning and the end the ever-
lasting friend.**

*Whatever... Are you robbing me or not? Why you got
that gun to my head?*

**I would never put a barrel to your head.
This is not a gun, son, but my finger of
righteousness.
I'm just pointing out who's blessed.**

**This may not seem like much but I just needed you
to raise your hands so I could show Satan who not to
touch. He can smell the pretenders.**

**Now he knows you're mine 'cause with a point of
my finger you were ready to surrender.**

And... I like it when you reach out to me.

It's like coming home to your child with outstretched arms yelling daddy.

That feels good to me.

And I see old Lu tried to remind you...
of you.

Well the wicked one is unworthy to stand witness.

Besides I can't remember anything you did before this morning...

when you asked me for forgiveness.

WE RIDE

While you're still waiting for signs long missed and forgotten.
The seals have been broken.
        Broken like the backs of blacks picking cotton stacks
                to killing kinfolks on corners.
I come to conquer.

       I, I am Conquest, often called Pestilence.

My seal was broken back before the world knew to keep score.
The end is always near.
I, and the white horse were first here, recall Cain and Able.

        I conquer wives with inferiority,
    families with alcohol, neighborhoods with drugs
        and natives with democracy.

I separate church from state,
can't have God getting in the way of what he sent me to do.
The trick is finding the slightest weakness
or difference in philosophy.
I got a group of chosen people fighting over who's the chosen
when I choose them all.

I keep closet doors closed
with fear of straight lines raised in judgment.
House nigga vs. field nigga, blue collar vs. white collar it's all the
             same to me.
        Willie Lynch is not who I claim to be
          but I did give him his recipe.

Ever notice how the Crips and Bloods, Republicans and
Democrats separate themselves with the same two colors?
       Those are my two favorite colors
      apparently they "red" my book of "blues".

I keep the boys in blue hating
                    those they pledged to protect and serve.
Pull the trigger click.
I'll even pause for a photo, but you'll never see me click.
          You're too busy consuming and dividing into cliques.
                You divide with the ease of single cell organisms,
                                  it's in your nature
                              you can't help yourself.

I divide poets with interstates slammed between them.
      I separate husbands from homes as easy as tearing meat from
                  bone forcing mothers to leave babies at home.
If I can't separate mother from child all it takes is a little crack.
              I smoke the competition.
                          This is the best of conquest,
                                the true pestilence.
                    Syphilis, herpes and HIV? Too easy.
                      The bubonic plague? Passé.
I conquer kings with greed, lay waste to leaders with their lust.

            I divide then conquer.
It takes a long time for a good ol'fashion biblical type
apocalypse to marinate, so I don't mind the wait.
              While you're listening for horse hooves from heaven,
                        we're riding Harleys and Hondas.
We stand hoping you're still waiting for our seals to be broken,
        blind to our movement we've been unleashed the words
            already spoken the book has been opened.

Though we be absent of his breath, and may not be men made
of mud merely, metaphors in the mind of a prophet's lucid
dream, we are here.
            We are real, we ride and our work has already begun.

Welcome to the end!

CURRICULUM VITAE
(ABOUT CHRISTOPHER MICHAEL)

1989   Learned how to write poetry

1999   Wrote a poem to impress a girl and discovered he was good at it.
Performed publicly at the Ying Yang in Atlanta Ga.
Introduced to Under One Roof and the Killeen Poetry Scene by Mr.
Nice
Entered his first poetry slam and won.

2004   Starts Slamming regularly at Austin Poetry Slam

2005   Wins the Austin City Grand Slam and makes the Austin Slam Team
Kicks off Killeen Poetry Slam with John Crow via The Poet's Ball

2006   Returns as the Austin Slam Champion and a member of the team
Released his first CD titled "The Appetizer"
Slam Champion Austin International Poetry Festival

2007   Killeen Poetry Slam makes its debut coached by Christopher
Michael at the National Poetry Slam missing national champions by
0.4 points bested by Team Charlotte (Dag Nabbit!!)
Comes in 2nd in the last National Individual Slam after a tie breaker
(Christopher may or may not still be bitter about that one)

2008   Killeen Slam Champion
Killeen Slam Team and coach

2009   Killeen Slam Team and coach
Rock The Republic Slam Champion

2010   Coaches Texas Youth Word Collectives Under 21 Slam
Arkansas Grand Slam Champion
Rock The Republic Slam Champion
Releases 2nd CD titled "Poet For Hire"
Killeen Slam Team

2011   After the tragic loss of Sheila Siobhan Christopher picks up the
leadership mantle of The Austin Youth Slam, now called "They
Speak" www.theyspeakaustin.org

2012   Returns to Austin Poetry Slam as coach, regular host and member
of the board.
They Speak Youth Slam Coach

2013   Attempts to take a break from poetry. FAILS!

2014   Austin Slam Team
        Kicks off his Think, Laugh, Cry Tour
        Elected to the Executive Council of Poetry Slam Inc.

2015   Finally writes a damn book!
        Maybe a new CD too.
        Winner 1st Texas Slam Master's Slam
        Slam Champion Austin International Poetry Festival
        Austin Neo Soul Slam Team

www.mrmichael310.com

@mrmichael310

Hootie Hooooo